DRAWINGS

DRAWINGS

by

VICCI SPERRY

ANDRÉ SAURET, ÉDITEUR

BOSTON BOOK AND ART SHOP, INC.

BOSTON, MASSACHUSETTS

Library of congress catalog card number 68-58697

PRINTED IN FRANCE

PREFACE

FROM earliest times man has expressed himself through the power of drawing.

When his needs changed and his feelings changed, it followed that the expression of his drawing changed.

From the beginning of civilization to the present times we have had a great history of art and of man's broad accomplishment in drawing. With the coming of the Renaissance the accomplishment of the artist as an individual burst into recognition. Also there was a developing compassion towards one's fellow man in the work of the artist—and this was reflected in his drawing.

This individuality and compassion reached superb heights in the drawings of Rembrandt. His work is a noble example of the power of drawing to express spontaneity, humanity, and skill with a glorious depth of space and feeling.

Drawing had become a major art form. It continued to be a living method of expression for all major artists up to our present time.

Through its long history, drawing has been used for ritual purposes, for language purposes, for practical communication, and for purely expressive purposes of fine art. Drawing as pure art, like all great art, knows no barriers of time, geography, race—and speaks a language to all nations and people.

In the final analysis, we might say it is the heart speaking to the heart—and thus it meets a timeless, universal need.

My own experience with drawing can be measured in many years and hundreds of drawings—drawings of the figure, drawings from nature, abstract drawings of space and form, and drawings of spacial abstract ideas.

Every experience has contributed to a deeper awareness of the relationship of space and form, of techniques, and most important, of that which is meaningful as art.

At the same time I was learning to dwell less on what I was seeing and more and more on qualities revealed by intuition, experience, and intelligence. I was learning to yield to qualities of tenderness and strength. Thought was released from precedented attitudes, and was opened to freshness, flow of space, and continuity.

Representation became based, not on realistic likeness, but on the reality of eternal qualities and of man's deep feelings of man caring for man. A greater expansiveness co-existed with a greater control and containment.

There is much in our day that argues cynicism and disillusionment, but always there are the many who react with artistic gratitude to the wonder of man and the glory of the universe. Ultimately, drawing as fine art, gathering inspiration from the artists of the past who have bequeathed us an art world, appears with an individual newness because of the infinite nature of its everlasting life source.

Vicci SPERRY

PLATES

1 - ARIADNE

"Art is dynamic and is never sustained within a finite static pattern."

Vivi Sperry

2 - THALIA

"The vitality settles into equilibrium, the expansiveness into all-inclusiveness."

3 - THE PIANIST

"When you think space first, what you say becomes more alive. Space being alive, it moves, and therefore appears on different planes."

4 - CLIO

"It matters not whether we express abstractly or representationally—
it is feeling and space that are our involvement."

5 - THE PICNIC

"The artist is deeply involved with space. He is making visible the space which seems to be invisible. When he gazes upon the sheet of paper, some magic is going on in his consciousness. He no longer sees a two-dimensional paper. He is entering a three-dimensional world."

6 - VASHTI

"All great art expression is involved with the control that gives the
freedom."

7 - ESTHER

"We are the reflection of infinity, therefore we are unlimited in our capacities.   We have ideas we never dreamed we had."

8 - CALIOPE

"The most dramatic contrast exists between the pure white and the
deepest black."

Vici Sperry

9 - CASSANDRA

"Each one sees differently. Also, each day each individual sees differently. This is the infinite variation and unfoldment of vision."

Vicki Sherry

10 - DIANA

"We are aware that we start with one idea, and we are aware of the fact that space is infinite—within this infinity, there can be no 'tightness.' There are no 'tight' spots in infinite space. We can soar, think, and move."

II - HECUBA

"We are unlimited in our capacity to feel movement. We are entering a world of space and at the same time we are working on one plane."

12 - ANDROMACHE

"Space, being alive,—it has no vacuums and no static area. Whatever we put into space reflects this aliveness and reveals the responding aliveness of the total space."

13 - REBEKAH

"The physical vision is involved with the appearance of temporal objects or scenes. The artist is involved with the eternal essence of objects and scenes and not with the temporal."

14 - THE MOTHER

"In drawing the figure with line, think of the line not as the outline of the figure but rather as that which is uniting the figure and the space. The line may be continuous or broken depending on the individual expression."

Vici Sperry

15 - THE FIRST DAUGHTER

"Art is the reflection of feeling in which everything is related to the total space."

16 - THE SECOND DAUGHTER

"A work of art gives one a feeling of reality which has a vitality of
organization and of lasting quality."

Vicci Sperry

17 - THE SON

"Dwelling on the total sense of space will help place the figure and the relationship of the parts of the figure."

18 - ZENOBIA

"Each one of us has the gift of individuality and, therefore, each one
of us has an individual style."

19 - THE BALLET DANCER

"Space is a living reality, nothing is inert within that living reality,
for good art is a reflection of life."

"The drawing of the features is never automatic, the lesser cannot take precedence over the greater. Therefore, the features, if portrayed, must serve the flow of the entire work."

21 - ATALANTA

"It is not representation that we seek, but the quality or essence of the experience."

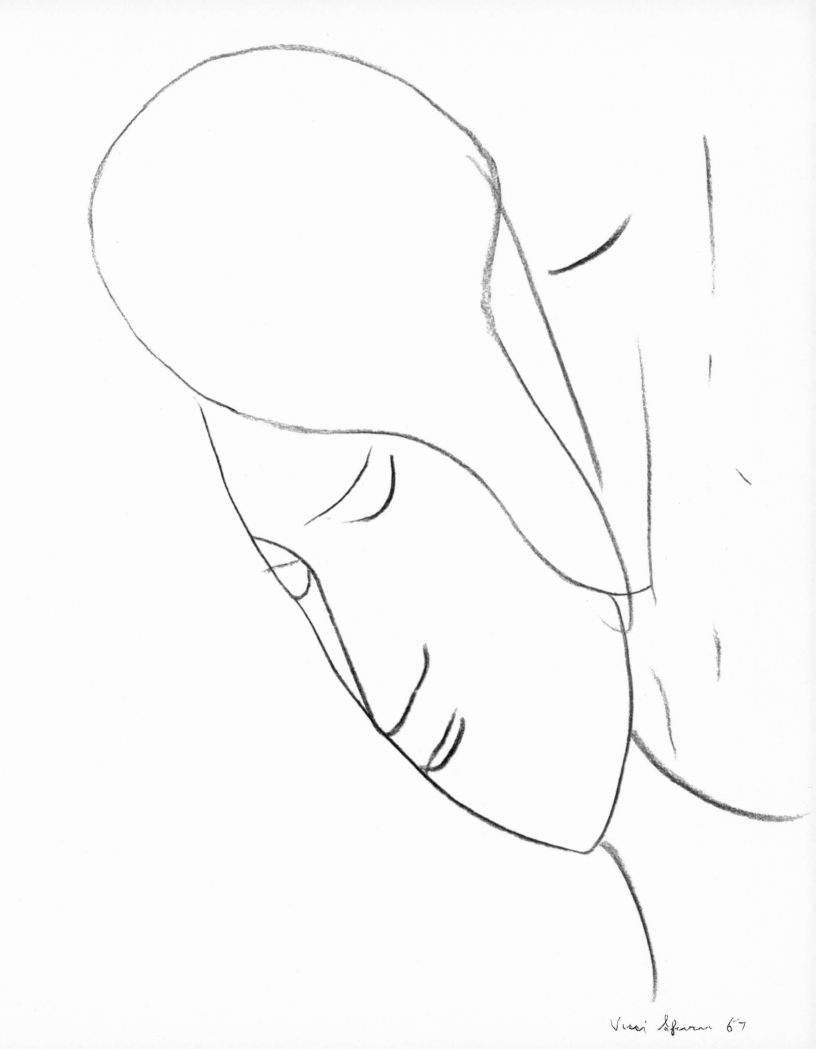

Vicci Sperry 67

22 - THE POETESS

"Dwelling too much on the appearances of objects may stop the flow
of movement."

23 - JOSEPH

"In all art experience, it is the vision and the understanding that is being developed. This prepares for the spontaneity of the expression."

Vicci Sperry

24 - *THE MUSICIAN*

"The great law is the law of continuity.   This continuity in movement in depth is not always obvious."

25 - OPHELIA

"Within the unlimited oneness, each element is related to the whole
and related to every other element."

"Thinking of infinity prevents crowdedness. There is nothing automatic in our vision. We are always seeing in a new way. No approach can become routine, for we always allow ourselves the freedom of a new way of seeing."

27 - SARAH

"Drawing invites the use of mass areas and of textures as well as line.
Encourage spontaneity, the joy of spontaneity, nothing laborious."

28 - NAOMI

"It is better to have a few lines that relate than a realism that violates
the totality of the form and the space."

"Spacial order, continuity of movement, movement of light, lead to
that which is more profound than the material representation—lead
to that which we call abstract qualities."

Vivi Skowry

30 - CERES

"When we feel everything related to the total space, all resolves into
a sense of equilibrium."

31 - ATHALIAH

"This should never become a static or routine approach, for at every moment of our development in art, it is necessary to work from feeling and intuition."

Vici Sperry

32 - PROSERPINA

"Our consciousness of starting from infinity gives us vitality and control."

33 - SARASVATI

"The beauty within each of us is that inner quality which gives forth radiance.   This is the opposite from the outward shell which cannot radiate beauty."

Vicci Sperry

34 - SOPHIA

"Be calm and allow the true self to blossom.   The inner self comes
forth with patience and gentleness.   In art, we can comprehend but
not always explain.   The same is true of life."

Vicci Sperry

35 - THETIS

"There can be a deeper reality of the subject matter that has evolved abstractly then of the subject matter that has evolved from the appearance."

36 - ALTHEA

"Feeling space helps to place and relate forms to the total composition."

37 - NIKE

"Calmness allows your native intuition to lead the way.   You will sense the pulsating, breathing quality entering the composition."

Vicc Shuvug

38 - ABIGAIL

"If you love what you are doing, the understanding is quickened.
You will not bring harshness to it."

Vince Sperry

39 - *HESTIA*

"Man will never cease to wonder at the beauty of the head."

"Blind impulsive action may make us feel as though we are doing something, but it will not lead us into the path of gentle understanding that makes for growth and true strength."

Vicki Sherry

41 - HANNAH

"Grandeur, life, and movement exist in the forms of space."

Vicci Sperry

42 - RHEA

"We are becoming more conscious of the total ensemble and its oneness. Everything contributes to the one idea."

43 - SELENE

"The macrocosm and the microcosm reflect the same world. It is the one spacial universe, the one energy, whether we are working on a small or a large canvas."

44 - *RUTH*

"The artist is sustained by using his native gift of intuition."

45 - DEBORAH

"First, we think of space.   Space is important because we live in it.
We breathe in it.   All ratios, proportion, and action are in space."

"The great artist lifts you into his world. Beauty is a reality. In the eloquent words of Ralph Waldo Emerson: 'For the world is not painted, or adorned, but is from the beginning beautiful; and God has not made some beautiful things, but Beauty is the creator of the universe.'"

47 - *KATHERINE*

"More and more we find infinite possibilities of our own development. Your own capacities are a constant revelation."

LIST OF DRAWINGS

All the quotations are from the second half of
"The Art Experience" by Vicci Sperry.

THIS BOOK,

WHICH WAS DESIGNED AND COMPILED
BY ANDRÉ SAURET, WAS FINISHED IN
OCTOBER 1969. THE REPRODUCTIONS
OF THE DRAWINGS WERE PRINTED
ON THE PRESSES OF THE IMPRIMERIE
MODERNE DU LION IN PARIS. THE
IMPRIMERIE DARANTIERE IN DIJON IS
RESPONSIBLE FOR THE TYPOGRAPHY.